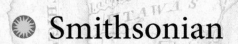

Smithsonian

Exploring
the
South Carolina
Colony

by Christin Ditchfield

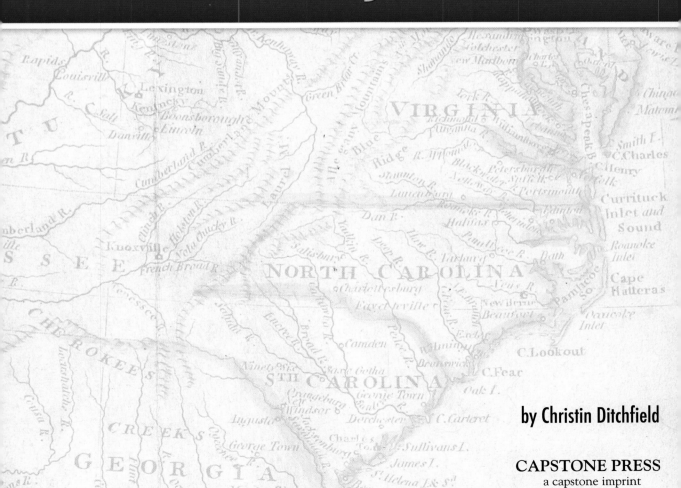

CAPSTONE PRESS
a capstone imprint

Smithsonian books are published by Capstone Press,
1710 Roe Crest Drive, North Mankato, Minnesota 56003
www.capstonepub.com

Library of Congress Cataloging-in-Publication Data
Ditchfield, Christin, author.
Title: Exploring the South Carolina Colony/by Christin Ditchfield.
Description: North Mankato, Minnesota: Capstone Press, [2017] |
   Series: Smithsonian. Exploring the 13 Colonies | Includes bibliographical references and index.
Audience: Ages 8–11
Identifiers: LCCN 2016005751
ISBN 9781515722304 (library binding)
ISBN 9781515722434 (paperback)
ISBN 9781515722564 (ebook PDF)
Subjects: LCSH: South Carolina—History—Colonial period, ca. 1600–1775—Juvenile literature.
South Carolina—History—1775–1865—Juvenile literature.
Classification: LCC F272 .D57 2017 | DDC 975.7/02—dc23
LC record available at http://lccn.loc.gov/2016005751

Editorial Credits
Jennifer Huston, editor; Richard Parker, designer; Eric Gohl, media researcher;
Kathy McColley, production specialist

Our very special thanks to Stephen Binns at the Smithsonian Center for Learning and Digital Access for
his curatorial review. Capstone would also like to thank Kealy Gordon, Smithsonian Institution Product
Development Manager, and the following at Smithsonian Enterprises: Christopher A. Liedel, President;
Carol LeBlanc, Senior Vice President; Brigid Ferraro, Vice President; Ellen Nanney, Licensing Manager.

Photo Credits
Alamy: historical-markers.org/Jason O. Watson, 35; Bridgeman Images: Ferens Art Gallery, Hull
Museums, UK, 17, © Look and Learn/Private Collection, 31, Peter Newark American Pictures/Private
Collection, 13; Capstone: 4, 14; Charleston Library Society, Charleston, SC: 37; CriaImages.com:
Jay Robert Nash Collection, 11 (bottom); David R. Wagner: 11 (top); Getty Images: Stringer/MPI, 6, 7,
12; Granger, NYC: 29; Library of Congress: 34 (right); National Guard Image Gallery: Don Troiani, 40;
Newscom: Heritage Images/The Print Collector, 18; New York Public Library: 38; North Wind Picture
Archives: cover, 8, 9, 21, 28, 30, 32, 33, 34 (left), 36, 39; Shutterstock: Joseph Sohm, 26–27, Natalia
Bratslavsky, 15; Wikimedia: Kmusser, 19, Nationalparks, 10, Public Domain, 5, 23, 24

Design Elements: Shutterstock

Printed and bound in the USA.
009669F16

Table of Contents

Introduction:
The 13 Colonies

In the early 1600s, many people left Europe to make better lives for themselves. By 1733 England had 13 Colonies in North America. A colony is a place settled by people from another country. People who move to a colony are still subject to the laws of their original homeland. The new country is like a "child" of the old country. The "parent" country is in charge and makes the rules. These 13 Colonies would become the United States of America.

Between 1607 and 1733, England established 13 Colonies in the present-day United States.

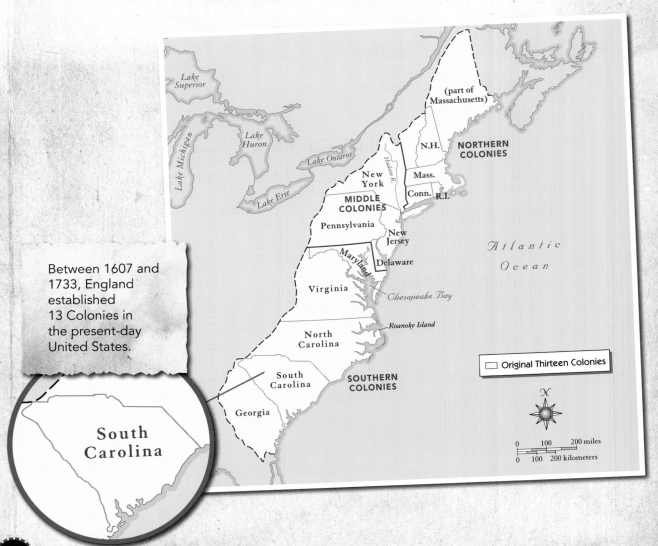

The king and queen of Spain hired Italian explorer Christopher Columbus (pictured here) to find a shortcut to Asia by sailing west across the Atlantic Ocean.

European Explorers in the Americas

America had first been discovered by Europeans in the 15th century. In 1492 explorer Christopher Columbus left Spain in an attempt to reach eastern Asia. He thought he could get there by sailing west across the Atlantic Ocean. He didn't realize that two continents—North and South America—were in the way! After a long ocean voyage, Columbus found himself on an island off the coast of North America. By accident he had stumbled upon a "New World."

After Columbus reached the New World, explorers from France, England, Spain, and other European countries soon followed. They brought back exciting stories of a wonderful land that was rich in **natural resources**. In the late 1500s, people from Europe began leaving their homelands to live there. Eventually, more people joined them and the 13 Colonies began to be formed.

Each of the colonies had its own unique characteristics. These differences stemmed from who settled there and why. Some were seeking religious freedom. Others wanted to get rich off the new land.

In 1607 Virginia became the first permanent English colony in North America. Other settlements soon followed as people from western Europe decided to make the New World their home.

Some of these **immigrants** were looking for fame and fortune. They hoped to find gold or other valuable resources that they could sell in Europe. Others simply wanted a fresh start in life. In some cases people were sent by their governments to claim the land and its resources for their home country. Others were trying to escape their governments. They wanted to live in a place where they were free to work and worship as they pleased.

Settlers in Virginia established the first permanent English colony in North America.

It wasn't easy to start a brand-new life in a strange land. The settlers could bring few of their belongings with them on the long ocean voyage. Along the way they suffered hardships, hunger, and disease. They risked everything to create a better future for themselves and their families.

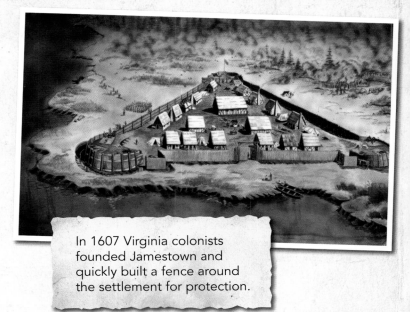

In 1607 Virginia colonists founded Jamestown and quickly built a fence around the settlement for protection.

The Original 13 Colonies

The first permanent European settlement in each colony:

Virginia	1607	Delaware	1638
Massachusetts	1620	Pennsylvania	1643
New Hampshire	1623	North Carolina	1653
New York	1624	New Jersey	1660
Connecticut	1633	South Carolina	1670
Maryland	1634	Georgia	1733
Rhode Island	1636		

Chapter 1:
South Carolina's Native People

When the first Europeans arrived, there were more than 30 different native tribes living in what would become the Carolina region. These included the Croatoans, Chicoras, Catawbas, Cherokees, and Yamasees. Many of these tribes lived at peace with one another. They were friends and allies. Other tribes were fierce enemies.

Manteo

Manteo was a member of the Croatoan tribe who became a great friend to the colonists of the Carolina region. He learned to speak English so that he could communicate with the settlers. He also helped keep the peace by resolving disagreements between the settlers and the Native Americans.

Manteo taught the settlers many things about the Croatoan culture and customs and the land on which they lived. He served as an interpreter and guide. Manteo was the first Native American **baptized** as a member of the Anglican Church or the Church of England.

The manner of their fishing.

Native Americans used spears to fish from their canoes.

Daily Life Among the Tribes

By the 1500s when Europeans began exploring the New World, native people had been living in North America for thousands of years. They had their own languages, customs, culture, and laws.

The men of the tribes hunted for deer, moose, bear, turkey, and rabbit. They used bows and arrows, spears, or traps to catch and kill their **prey**. They also fished in the rivers and streams. Tribes living near the ocean caught oysters, clams, and lobsters.

Native American women took care of the home. They also grew corn, beans, pumpkins, and squash. While working in the fields, Native American mothers carried their babies on their backs.

Women of the tribe also gathered wild rice that grew along the banks of rivers and streams. This rice was used to make many kinds of soup and stew.

By the time the first Europeans arrived, Native Americans had been harvesting corn for thousands of years. They taught the early settlers how to grow the crop and use it for food.

baptize—to admit into the Christian faith with a spiritual ceremony

prey—an animal hunted by another animal for food

Native American children gathered firewood and helped in the fields. They also collected nuts and wild berries.

Some tribes lived in dome-shaped homes called wigwams. Other tribes built homes called longhouses that looked like long, narrow cabins. The frames were made of tree branches and were covered with large strips of bark. Several families lived in each longhouse.

When the weather was warm, the Native Americans wore light clothing made of leaves, long grasses, or other plant fibers. In cooler weather men wore shirts and leggings made from animal skins. They also wore breechcloths, which looked like aprons, with front and back flaps hanging from a belt at the waist. Women wore long dresses that were often decorated with shells, paint, or porcupine quills.

Some tribes of the Carolina region lived in wigwams made by weaving long grass, reeds, or sheets of tree bark into mats. The mats covered frames made of arched poles.

On special occasions Native American men, women, and children decorated their bodies with paint. They also wore jewelry made of shells or bones and headdresses made of feathers. Both men and women had piercings and tattoos.

Many Native Americans wore clothing made from deerskin. They also decorated their bodies with feathers, paint, and jewelry.

Critical Thinking with Primary Sources

John White was an English artist and explorer. His drawings of the Carolina region gave Europeans their first glimpse of what Native Americans and the North American landscape looked like. What does this picture tell you about Native American villages and the people living there? In what ways might historians use White's drawings today?

Arrival of the Colonists

When the colonists arrived, they brought with them all kinds of things that the Native Americans had never seen before. They brought new weapons, such as guns, plus tools, fabrics, and other household items. The tribes found that the settlers were eager to trade these items for food, land, and lumber. The settlers also wanted animal furs that they could send back to Europe and sell for a lot of money.

In peaceful times the Native Americans taught the settlers many things. They showed the newcomers how to plant and harvest a wide variety of fruits and vegetables. They knew how to make these crops grow successfully. The natives also knew which plants could be used as medicines.

Colonists from Jamestown were eager to trade with local Native American tribes.

Some Native Americans mixed their customs and clothing style with those of the Europeans they met.

Over time the Native Americans adopted some European customs and culture. Many learned to speak English, French, or Spanish. They also learned to read and write, which helped them create a written record of their own languages, cultures, and histories.

Unfortunately the Europeans also brought with them diseases, such as **smallpox** and **yellow fever**. These illnesses sometimes wiped out entire tribes. In addition the tribes and settlers often fought over land. The Native Americans were not happy that the colonists were taking away their land and hunting grounds. Sometimes their disputes led to war. Within 100 years of the arrival of Europeans, the Native American population of South Carolina was nearly wiped out.

smallpox—a disease that spreads easily from person to person, causing chills, fever, and pimples that scar

yellow fever—an illness that can cause high fever, chills, nausea, and kidney and liver failure; liver failure causes the skin to become yellow,

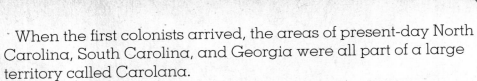

Chapter 2:
A New Colony

When the first colonists arrived, the areas of present-day North Carolina, South Carolina, and Georgia were all part of a large territory called Carolana.

The first colonists observed that the area now known as South Carolina was a rich land, full of natural beauty. With mountains, rolling hills and valleys, thick forests, and rivers, streams, and swamps, wildlife was and still is plentiful in the area. The colonists soon discovered that South Carolina's warm, humid climate and flat fertile lands were perfect for growing rice and cotton.

In the early 1500s, Spanish explorers built several settlements in South Carolina, but none of them lasted very long. The Spanish fought with the Native Americans and with each other. When the explorers ran out of food and supplies, many of them died. The Spanish decided to focus their efforts on Florida instead.

South Carolina's regions are very different. Beaches and palm trees dot the coast. The northwestern part of the state has rolling hills and mountains.

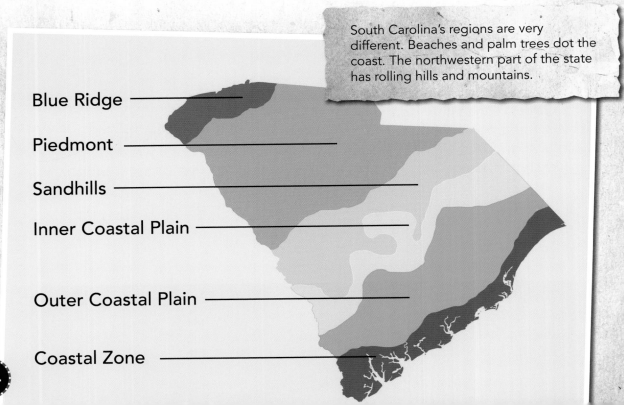

Blue Ridge

Piedmont

Sandhills

Inner Coastal Plain

Outer Coastal Plain

Coastal Zone

The French also tried to establish colonies in South Carolina, but they failed too. Then in 1584 an Englishman named Sir Walter Raleigh sent a scouting party to the area. His explorers returned with wonderful reports of this new land. They thought it would be an excellent place to start a new colony for England.

But more than 20 years passed before the first successful English settlement was built farther north in Jamestown, Virginia. By 1640 there were nearly 26,000 Europeans living in the American Colonies.

Further inland, South Carolina is home to lush, green forests full of plants, wildlife, and waterfalls.

"*Deer in abundance, bigger and better meat [than] ours in England ... Elkes of a large size ... Beasts of prey, that are profitable for their Furres, as Bevers, Otters, Foxes, ... Fowle of all sorts, Partridges and wild Turkies 100 in a flock ... Fish there are in great abundance, of all sorts.*"

—a Carolina colonist describes the area in a 1649 letter to friends in England

Some of these people began to move south into the region known as Carolana. England's King Charles I had assigned this land to Sir Robert Heath in 1629. However, Heath failed to start a successful settlement there, so in 1663, King Charles II reclaimed the land. He changed its name to Carolina and gave it to eight **proprietors**, or landlords. These men were given the authority to build settlements, organize armies, and collect taxes.

South Carolina's First Permanent Settlement

In March 1670 the first group of about 100 English settlers arrived on the shores of present-day South Carolina. They built a settlement that they called Charles Town. They chose a location where ships could dock and goods could be sent downriver. Over the next 100 years, South Carolina became home to immigrants from England, Ireland, Scotland, Wales, and Germany.

Once settlers began to arrive, the proprietors appointed a governor. They had already created a system of laws called the Fundamental Constitutions of Carolina. This gave the colonists many rights as well as many rules to follow.

> *"[W]e returned, viewing the Land on both sides [of] the River, and found as good tracts of land, dry, well wooded, pleasant and delightful as we have seen any where in the world ..."*
>
> —Captain William Hilton's description of what he saw while exploring the Carolana coast in 1663

In the 1700s Charles Town was one of the busiest seaports in America.

One important right was the freedom of religion, which meant that people from all faiths were welcome in Carolina. This was one reason many people were willing to leave their homes in Europe. In England, for example, people who did not belong to the official Church of England were often **persecuted**. Many people thought this was unfair, so they came to America where they could practice their religion of choice.

In 1680 there were 1,000 colonists living in Carolina. That same year the Charles Town settlement moved nearby to a place between the Ashley and Cooper Rivers. This new location proved ideal for trade and was also easier to defend from attacks by Native Americans and pirates. This permanent settlement eventually became known as Charleston, and it is now the oldest city in South Carolina.

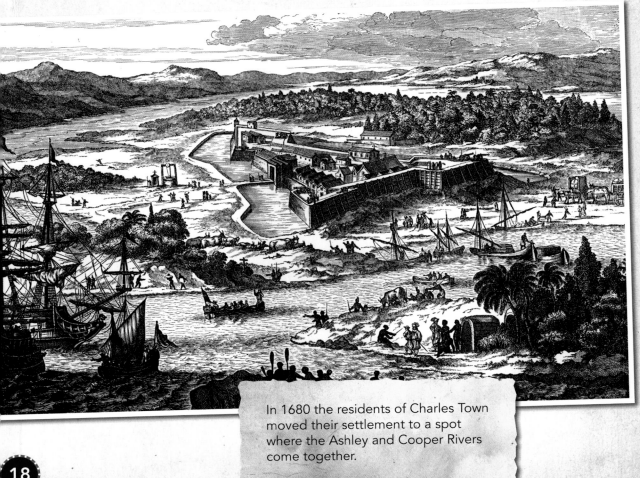

In 1680 the residents of Charles Town moved their settlement to a spot where the Ashley and Cooper Rivers come together.

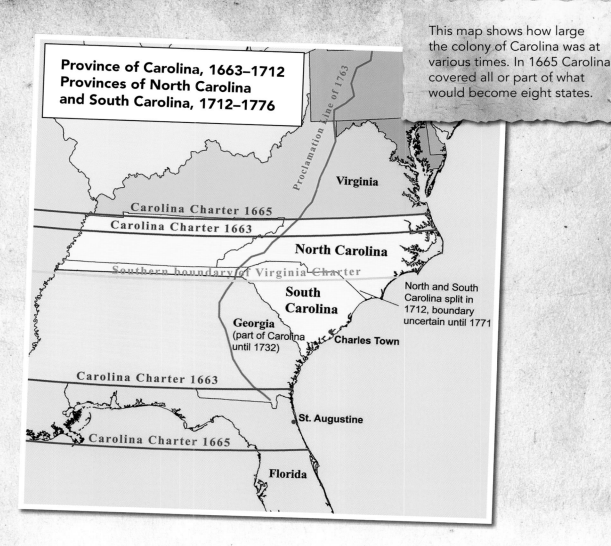

This map shows how large the colony of Carolina was at various times. In 1665 Carolina covered all or part of what would become eight states.

Province of Carolina, 1663–1712
Provinces of North Carolina and South Carolina, 1712–1776

Proclamation Line of 1763

Virginia

Carolina Charter 1665

Carolina Charter 1663

North Carolina

Southern boundary of Virginia Charter

South Carolina

North and South Carolina split in 1712, boundary uncertain until 1771

Georgia (part of Carolina until 1732)

Charles Town

Carolina Charter 1663

St. Augustine

Carolina Charter 1665

Florida

A Colony Divided

In 1712 North Carolina and South Carolina became separate colonies. However, the king and the English government were not happy with the job that the proprietors were doing. South Carolina was more valuable to England because of its natural resources. So in 1719 South Carolina was taken away from the proprietors and became a **royal colony**. This meant that it was ruled directly by the king. In 1729 the king took control of North Carolina as well.

persecute—to continually treat in a cruel and unfair way
royal colony—a colony controlled by a monarch

Chapter 3:
Challenges and Changes in South Carolina

By the late 1600s, the population of Carolina was growing rapidly. But tragedy struck in 1698. That year Charles Town's population was nearly wiped out by a fire, a hurricane, and a smallpox **epidemic**. The following year a yellow fever outbreak killed 150 residents in a matter of days.

> *"We have had the small pox amongst us nine or ten months which [has] been very infectious and mortal. We have lost … 200 or 300 persons. And on the 24 February a fire broke out in the night in Charles Town which [has] burnt the dwellings … of at least fifty families."*

—Governor Joseph Blake in a letter to the proprietors, March 12, 1698

Did You Know?

In 1702 France and Spain began fighting the English for control of North America. This was known as Queen Anne's War. In 1706 French and Spanish troops attempted to take over Charles Town. Although the town was battling a yellow fever epidemic, members of the **militia** rallied and were waiting for the invaders. After four days of skirmishes, the invaders sailed away in defeat.

American Uprisings

From the time the first colonists arrived, relations with the Native Americans were uneasy. Over the years, as more and more settlers arrived in the American Colonies, the natives were pushed off their lands. This made them very unhappy. Their anger turned violent in April 1715 when Yamasee tribe members attacked and killed 90 white settlers in southeastern South Carolina.

During the Yamasee War, Native Americans and colonists engaged in deadly battles over land and hunting grounds.

For the next two years, Carolina militiamen battled the Yamasees, Catawbas, and other tribes who wanted to rid the area of white settlers. Colonists from outside of Charles Town abandoned their farms and fled to the city. Soon there was a shortage of food in Charles Town, and the colonists were in danger of starving.

But then warriors from the powerful Cherokee tribe agreed to help the people of South Carolina in exchange for weapons and other goods. Colonists from neighboring Virginia also came to South Carolina's aid. Together they pushed the Yamasees south to Florida. There they combined with runaway slaves and other Native Americans to form the Seminole tribe. By the time the Yamasee War came to an end, hundreds of settlers and Native Americans had died.

epidemic—an infectious disease that spreads quickly through a community or population group

militia—a group of volunteer citizens who are organized to fight but are not professional soldiers

Villains on the Seas

As an important seaport town, Charles Town was in constant danger of pirate raids during Colonial times. Because of his cruel and sneaky tactics, the most feared pirate of the day was Edward Teach. He gained the nickname Blackbeard because of his long, jet-black beard, which he tied with colorful ribbons. To add to his ferocious look, he wore lit matches in his hair.

In May 1718 Blackbeard and his fearsome crew sailed into Charles Town Harbor. After looting several ships docked in the harbor, they took a number of passengers hostage and held them for ransom. Typically pirates conducted raids in search of gold, silver, and jewels. But this time Blackbeard and his men wanted something different—medical supplies.

After a six-day standoff, Blackbeard was ready to kill the hostages. But at the last minute, the townspeople of Charles Town came through with the medical supplies. The pirates released the hostages and sailed off without firing a shot. But not before they robbed the hostages of their money and jewelry.

> *"[His] beard was black ... of an extravagant length; ... He was accustomed to twist it with ribbons, in small tails ... and turn them about his ears ... [He] stuck lighted matches under his hat, which ... his eyes naturally looking fierce and wild ... that imagination cannot form an idea of a Fury ... to look more frightful."*
>
> —Captain Charles Johnson, *A General History of the Robberies and Murders of the Most Notorious Pyrates*

The fearsome Blackbeard led other pirates raiding ships and killing their crews along the coast of Colonial America.

The End of Blackbeard's Reign of Terror

In the fall of 1718, Blackbeard and his men were on Ocracoke Island, off the Carolina coast. They had no idea that Robert Maynard of the Royal Navy had been sent to capture them.

Blackbeard's life came to an end in 1718 during a dramatic duel with Robert Maynard of the Royal Navy.

On November 22 Maynard caught up with Blackbeard and his crew. Blackbeard's men fired a hail of gunfire at Maynard's ship. Within seconds 21 of Maynard's crew were injured or dead.

Thinking that they'd won the battle, Blackbeard and his men went aboard Maynard's ship to finish off the crew. Suddenly Maynard and several men charged the pirates from below deck.

With swords and pistols drawn, Blackbeard and Maynard engaged in hand-to-hand combat. Blackbeard fired at Maynard but missed. Maynard shot back and hit Blackbeard in the shoulder. Still able to swing his sword, the pirate knocked a knife from Maynard's hand. As Maynard prepared to shoot Blackbeard again, one of Maynard's men came from behind and slashed Blackbeard's throat. The great pirate was dead.

Anne Bonny (1698–1782)

Born in Ireland, Anne Bonny moved to South Carolina with her parents as a young girl. In 1720 she fell in love with the pirate John Rackham, also known as "Calico Jack." Bonny joined Calico Jack as he and his crew raided ships on the high seas. Another female pirate, Mary Read, was also part of Calico Jack's crew. They participated in the violent raids, but they disguised themselves as men.

In late 1720 the governor of the Bahamas sent Captain Jonathan Barnet to capture the pirates. On November 15 Barnet caught up with Calico Jack and his crew. Bonny and Read put up a fierce fight, but they were captured with the rest of the crew. Calico Jack and the male pirates were found guilty of piracy and were hanged. Bonny and Read were found guilty as well, but because they were both pregnant, their lives were spared. Read died in prison a year later. When Bonny was released from prison, she returned to Charles Town. She later married, had more children, and lived a long life.

Chapter 4:
Prosperous Times

By 1760 Charles Town was the wealthiest city in the Southern Colonies. But when the first colonists arrived in what is now South Carolina, they struggled to survive. The climate and the soil were different from their homeland. It was only with the help of Native Americans that the early colonists were able to make it. The Native Americans gave them food when they ran out and taught them how to farm the unfamiliar land.

These first colonists grew corn and tobacco. But in the mid-1680s, the colonists discovered that rice grew very well in the colony's hot, wet climate. Rice quickly became South Carolina's **cash crop**. By 1720 the colony's planters were producing more than 20 million pounds of rice per year.

"It [Charles Town] far surpasses all I ever saw, or expected to see, in America."
—Bostonian Josiah Quincy, Jr. describing his visit to Charles Town in 1773

Another important crop in Colonial South Carolina was indigo, a plant used to make blue dye. At the time blue dye was only made in Asian countries, such as India. Because it had to be imported, only the richest people wore blue clothing. All that changed in the 1740s when Eliza Lucas raised the first successful crop of indigo in America.

While her father was away in the military, Eliza was left in charge of his three South Carolina **plantations**. During this time she experimented with growing several new crops, including ginger, alfalfa, and indigo. After several years experimenting with indigo, she finally had success. Soon South Carolina had another cash crop. By 1754 a million pounds of indigo were being exported from South Carolina each year. But who was going to do the hard work of farming all these crops?

Drayton Hall near Charleston is one of the few plantation homes in South Carolina to survive both the Revolutionary War (1775–1783) and the Civil War (1861–1865).

"I make no doubt Indigo will prove a very valuable Commodity in time ..."

—Eliza Lucas, in a letter to her father, June 4, 1741

cash crop—a crop that is grown to be sold rather than for use by the farmer

plantation—a large farm where crops are grown

Chapter 5:
Slave Labor

By the 1720s rice was South Carolina's most profitable crop. The colony's planters knew they could make a fortune selling their crops. But it took a lot of hard work to plant, grow, and harvest rice and later, indigo and cotton. The landowners could not do it alone, even with the help of servants and other paid workers. So they used slaves—people they could force to work without pay.

Slavery in the New World

The Spanish first captured Native Americans and forced them to work as slaves. But many of them quickly died from European diseases, so the Spanish started bringing slaves from Africa. Some were captured and kidnapped. Others were sold into slavery by enemy tribes. It wasn't long before other countries were making money from the African slave trade.

African slaves endured the worst conditions imaginable as they made the long ocean voyage to America. Hundreds of people were chained together below deck where they could barely move or breathe. They had no fresh air, no toilets, and very little food. Many died of sickness, starvation, or **suffocation**. Some jumped from the ship and drowned themselves rather than live as slaves.

Slaves toiled in the hot, sticky air to collect rice. In Colonial times more rice was produced in South Carolina than in any other colony. By 1700 South Carolina was exporting more than 400,000 pounds of rice each year.

Critical Thinking with Primary Sources

In Colonial America most slaves were captured or kidnapped Africans who were forced into unpaid labor. Many worked long hours performing backbreaking work on large plantations in the South. What is the first thing you notice about this advertisement? What do you think would be the hardest part of life as a slave?

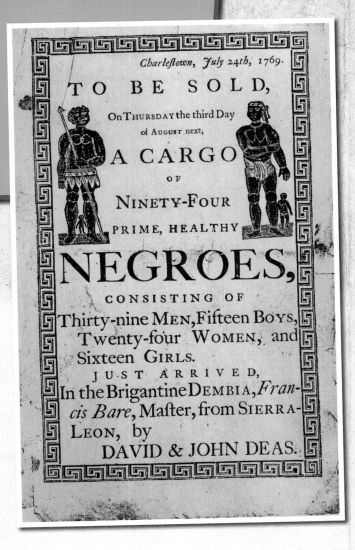

Charlestown, July 24th, 1769.

TO BE SOLD,

On THURSDAY the third Day of AUGUST next,

A CARGO

OF

NINETY-FOUR

PRIME, HEALTHY

NEGROES,

CONSISTING OF

Thirty-nine MEN, Fifteen BOYS, Twenty-four WOMEN, and Sixteen GIRLS.

JUST ARRIVED,

In the Brigantine DEMBIA, *Francis Bare*, Master, from SIERRA-LEON, by

DAVID & JOHN DEAS.

When they arrived in America, slaves were sold to wealthy landowners. Slaves were forced to work from sunrise to sunset, six days a week. They were often beaten with whips or chains if they worked too slowly or if they displeased their masters in any way. Most slaves were given very little food, clothing, or shelter.

One-third of the slaves in South Carolina died within three years after leaving Africa. This was likely due to poor diet and harsh working conditions. Working in the fields was physically very difficult and exhausting. Also, rice is grown in wet, swampy areas—the perfect climate for disease-carrying mosquitoes.

suffocate—to die from a lack of air or oxygen

Some masters treated their slaves better than others did. They gave their slaves adequate food, housing, and medical care. Slaves were sometimes allowed to grow fruits and vegetables that they could sell to one day purchase their freedom. Some slaves were set free when their master died.

"Only those negroes kept for house-service are better cared for ... But they who have the largest droves keep them the worst, let them run naked mostly or in rags, and accustom them as much as possible to hunger, but exact of them steady work."

—Johann David Schöpf, a visitor to the 13 Colonies, observing a slave auction

Slaves who worked inside a master's home were treated much better than those who worked in the fields.

The Stono Rebellion

In the early 1700s, African slaves made up more than two-thirds of South Carolina's population. As poorly as most slaves were treated, it's not surprising that many tried to run away.

On September 9, 1739, a group of runaway slaves gathered near the Stono River outside Charles Town. They planned to head south toward Florida, where they thought they would be free. First they stopped at a store, stole some guns and ammunition, and killed two shopkeepers. As the group continued on, it grew to nearly 100 slaves. They killed any white people they encountered.

Fed up with their poor living and working conditions, slaves in South Carolina revolted in 1739.

By the end of the next day, a group of colonists caught up with the runaway slaves. They exchanged gunfire and 30 slaves were killed. The rest of the runaways escaped but were captured and hanged during the following months.

After the Stono Rebellion, the colonists were terrified that other revolts would break out. They quickly passed laws making it illegal for slaves to gather in groups, travel without permission, or earn their own money. The colonists hoped this would stop further rebellions because South Carolina's economy could not survive without slave labor. It was mainly due to the backbreaking labor of slaves that South Carolina had become the wealthiest of the 13 Colonies.

Chapter 6:

Life in Colonial South Carolina

South Carolina was one of the fastest-growing of the 13 Colonies in the 1700s. Many settlers came from England, France, Germany, Ireland, and Scotland. Most were planters, but as towns and cities sprang up, merchants, tailors, and other craftsmen found work. By purchasing from these skilled craftsmen, colonists no longer had to import clothing, furniture, and other household items from England. They could buy what they needed in any of the 13 Colonies.

Some wealthy families still bought the most expensive clothing and furniture from England. They built large mansions on their plantations. Servants and slaves took care of the housework, as well as the farming. For entertainment the wealthy enjoyed musical performances, dancing, the theater, and horse races.

Children of wealthy parents were taught by tutors or sent to private schools in Charles Town. Older children went to Europe to attend fine universities.

By the 1700s colonists in larger cities were able to buy whatever they needed in town rather than having items imported from Europe.

Did You Know?

Founded in 1732 the *South Carolina Gazette* was the first newspaper in America to have a female publisher. Elizabeth Timothy took over running the newspaper when her husband died in 1738. She ran the paper until 1746 when her son became publisher at age 21.

In Colonial families everyone had chores to do. The girl pictured here is peeling apples to help her mother make a pie.

Other families lived more simply. Everyone worked together to care for the home, farm, or family business. Even young children had chores to do.

On smaller farms boys helped their fathers with the planting and harvesting. Some young boys left home to work as apprentices and learn a trade from a master craftsman. In exchange for his training, an apprentice lived and worked in the craftsman's shop.

Girls helped their mothers with household tasks, such as cooking and sewing. They also churned butter, washed clothes, and took care of their younger brothers and sisters.

Because there weren't many schools during Colonial times, parents taught their children to read and write at home. For fun, girls played with dolls made out of rags, straw, or wooden spoons. Boys often went hunting with their fathers. Children also played games such as checkers and dominoes. At night families gathered around the fireplace to tell stories, sing songs, or play instruments.

Religion in Colonial South Carolina

South Carolina was settled by people from many different ethnic and religious groups. Even so, most residents of Colonial South Carolina were Protestants, including Anglicans, Quakers, Presbyterians, and French Huguenots.

South Carolina was also home to a handful of Catholics and Jews. Like many people who came to America during this time, they came to escape persecution in their home countries.

Colonial families often gathered around the fireplace at night. In this painting, the men play instruments while the women work at a spinning wheel.

By 1700 about 450 French Huguenots had settled in South Carolina. Their current church (pictured here) dates back to 1845. It survived destruction during the Civil War and an earthquake in 1886.

Francis Salvador (1747–1776)

After the Revolutionary War, the Jewish population in South Carolina grew rapidly. By 1800 there were more Jews in South Carolina than any other place in America. Unlike many colonies South Carolina allowed Jews to hold public office. Francis Salvador was elected to South Carolina's Provincial Congress in 1774 and again in 1775. In 1776 he was the first Jewish soldier to die in the Revolutionary War.

In the 1730s and 1740s, a religious movement known as the "Great Awakening" spread throughout the American Colonies. Preachers such as Jonathan Edwards and George Whitefield gave lively, emotional sermons on the need to turn away from wrong deeds and follow God. They convinced Christian people that a personal relationship with God was more important than church rituals. They also preached that each person is responsible for his or her own actions and that all people are equal in the eyes of God. These teachings may have helped inspire some colonists to fight for their freedom during the American Revolution.

Did You Know?

Charleston's Huguenot Church traces its roots back to the 1680s, making it the oldest continuously active Huguenot congregation in the United States. The church is nicknamed "The Church of the Tides" because in Colonial times, services were timed according to the tides. Settlers from plantations along the coast rode to church in boats carried along by the tide.

Chapter 7:
The Road to Revolution and Statehood

In 1754 Great Britain and France went to war in North America over control of land there. Some Native American tribes fought for the French, while others backed the British. The colonists sided with Britain, their "mother country." After winning the French and Indian War in 1763, **Parliament** taxed the colonists to pay for the conflict.

Taxes placed on sugar, tea, newspapers, playing cards, and other everyday items made the colonists furious. They believed they should not pay taxes unless they were allowed to participate in Parliament. They wanted a say in any decisions that affected their daily lives.

Many of South Carolina's leaders joined a group called the Sons of Liberty to protest the Stamp Act and other unfair laws. They also **boycotted** the taxed goods, hoping it would force the king to put an end to the unfair taxes. The Stamp Act was **repealed** in 1766. However, a year later Parliament issued the Townshend Acts, which placed taxes on glass, paper, tea, paint, and lead. After that the colonists began boycotting all British goods.

In 1773 colonists in Boston staged a memorable protest against the tea tax. They boarded a British ship in Boston Harbor and dumped 340 chests of tea overboard. This event became known as the Boston Tea Party.

American colonists were not happy being taxed by Great Britain. Many, like the woman shown here, took out their anger on the tax collectors.

Realizing that the problems with Great Britain could not be resolved peacefully, the colonists started talking about forming their own independent nation. In 1774 South Carolina created its own independent government, the Provincial Congress. Two years later South Carolina and the rest of the 13 Colonies officially declared their independence from Great Britain. They were prepared to go to war and fight for their freedom.

Critical Thinking with Primary Sources

A year after the Boston Tea Party, a similar event occurred in Charles Town. In early November 1774, the British ship *Britannia* pulled into Charles Town Harbor carrying passengers from London. Also on board were seven chests of tea that were subject to a hefty tax. The merchants who purchased the tea were ordered to dump it overboard. According to the *South Carolina Gazette* article below, eyewitnesses heard "three hearty Cheers after the emptying of each Chest."

Why do you think the merchants were ordered to dump the tea they bought? Do you think this was a good way to protest the tea tax? What are some other ways the colonists could have protested the tea tax?

CHARLES-TOWN, NOVEMBER 7.

"… On Thursday at Noon, an Oblation was made to Neptune, of the said seven chests of Tea, by Messrs. Lindsay, Kinsley and Mackenzie themselves; who going on board the Ship in the Stream, with their own Hands respectively stove the Chests belong to each, and emptied their Contents into the River, in the Presence of the Committee of Observation, who likewise went on board, and in View of the whole General Committee on the Shore besides numerous Concourse of People, who gave three hearty Cheers after the emptying of each Chest, and immediately after separated as if nothing had happened."

The Revolutionary War in South Carolina

During the Revolutionary War (1775–1783), South Carolina was bitterly divided between **Loyalists** and **Patriots**. During the war more than 200 battles and skirmishes were fought in South Carolina. Charles Town Harbor was a key location that both the Americans and the British fought to control. The British attempted to capture Charles Town several times during the war. One attempt came in June 1776, when the British Navy got as far as Sullivan's Island in Charles Town Harbor. Colonel William Moultrie and his troops were waiting for them. After exchanging gunfire and cannonballs for nearly 12 hours, the British gave up and sailed away.

The British finally succeeded in taking Charles Town in 1780. In April of that year, the British Army began an attack on Charles Town. At the same time, the British Navy sailed into Charles Town Harbor. After battling the British for six weeks, the Americans surrendered on May 12. The British took more than 3,000 Patriots as prisoners of war. They also captured a large quantity of weapons and ammunition. It was the worst defeat of the Revolutionary War for the Americans.

The "Swamp Fox" Francis Marion (1732–1795)

After the fall of Charles Town in 1780, General Francis Marion took over a troop of South Carolina militiamen. They were known for using **guerilla warfare** to surprise the enemy. By hiding in forests or even swamps, Marion and his men often defeated larger units of British troops. Using these tactics Marion's group once rescued 150 American prisoners of war.

Although Marion never led his troops into a major battle, his trickery and craftiness played a significant role in keeping the Patriots in the war. Mel Gibson's character in the movie *The Patriot* was based on Francis Marion and his comrade Thomas Sumter.

The Tide Turns

The loss of Charles Town only made the Patriots fight harder. In October 1780 Major Patrick Ferguson and a band of 1,100 Loyalists positioned themselves on a large hill known as Kings Mountain. The Patriots charged and surrounded the Loyalists. Refusing to surrender, Ferguson led his men down the hillside where they were cut down by the Patriots. Nearly all of the Loyalists were wounded, captured, or killed. With only 28 Patriots killed, the battle was a turning point for the Americans that greatly boosted their spirits. Thomas Jefferson recalled the battle in an 1822 letter. He said, "it was the joyful [announcement] of that turn of the tide of success which terminated the revolutionary war, with the seal of our independence."

During the Battle of Kings Mountain, British commander Patrick Ferguson led a group of Loyalists against 900 militiamen.

Did You Know?

After the British seized Charles Town, the captured Patriot weapons were stored in a building in the city. One of the loaded weapons went off, which sparked a massive explosion. More than 5,000 muskets fired all at once, and 180 barrels of gunpowder exploded. Six houses were destroyed in the explosion, and nearly 200 people were killed.

Loyalist—a colonist who was loyal to Great Britain during the Revolutionary War
Patriot—a person who sided with the colonies during the Revolutionary War
guerilla warfare—a type of military action using small groups of fighters to carry out surprise attacks against enemy forces

The Patriots scored another important victory at the Battle of Cowpens in January 1781. During the noise and confusion of the battle, the Patriot troops thought their commander had ordered them to surrender. Thinking they had won, the British began leaving the battlefield. When the commander rallied the Patriots to continue, they surrounded the British, who quickly surrendered. In less than an hour, the Patriots captured more than 500 enemy soldiers and killed 110. It was reported that the Patriots lost only 12 men in the battle.

During 1780 and 1781, Patriot troops led by Francis Marion and Nathanael Greene pushed the British out of the Carolinas and into Virginia. By the time the British made it back to Yorktown, Virginia, they were tired and worn out. British General Charles Cornwallis had lost many men and was nearly out of supplies. The Americans easily captured the British and forced them to surrender. It was the last major battle of the Revolutionary War. The colonists had won their independence!

After some moments of confusion during the Battle of Cowpens, Patriot troops rallied to victory.

A New Nation

The war was over, but the boycotts, trade restrictions, and interruption of business had taken their toll on South Carolina's economy. South Carolina residents had lost a lot of money during the fight for independence. It would take decades for the state to recover financially.

Emily Geiger (1765–1825)

During the summer of 1781, Patriot General Nathanael Greene wanted to send a message to another Patriot general, Thomas Sumter. Greene wanted to work with Sumter to plan an attack on British General Lord Rawdon and his troops. However, the area between Greene and Sumter was full of Loyalists, and none of Greene's men would volunteer for the dangerous mission. Instead a teenage girl named Emily Geiger volunteered to deliver the message.

During the mission Geiger was stopped by scouts for the British Army. They sent for a woman to search her. When no one was looking, Geiger ate the letter from General Greene. The scouts couldn't find any reason to hold her, so they let her go. Geiger continued on her journey and gave the message to Sumter in person—she had memorized it.

With the war over, the United States was officially an independent nation. But the new country needed a permanent system of government. In September 1787 representatives from 12 of the 13 Colonies drafted the U.S. Constitution. (Rhode Island did not send representatives to the Constitutional Convention.) But there were many arguments and disagreements. The smaller colonies worried that the larger colonies would have more power.

South Carolina was particularly concerned that the Northern Colonies would create laws that would cause hardships for them. The biggest issue was slavery. The Southern Colonies depended on slaves to work their farms and plantations. They wanted to make sure that slavery would remain legal. Eventually the other representatives agreed to respect the Southern Colonies' wishes. However, over time, many Northern Colonies did ban slavery.

On May 23, 1788, representatives from South Carolina **ratified** the new U.S. Constitution. South Carolina became the eighth state to join the United States of America.

ratify—to formally approve a document

Timeline

1492 Christopher Columbus arrives in the Americas.

1521 Spanish sea captain Francisco Gordillo lands on the coast of what is now South Carolina.

1540 Hernando de Soto searches the Carolina region for gold.

1562 French explorer Jean Ribault establishes a settlement at Port Royal.

1629 King Charles I gives a large area of southern Virginia (also known as Carolana) to Sir Robert Heath.

1663 King Charles II renames the land Carolina and divides it among eight proprietors, or landlords.

1670 Charles Town is established. It is the first permanent European settlement in South Carolina.

1698 Charles Town is nearly destroyed by a fire, a powerful hurricane, and an outbreak of smallpox.

1712 North Carolina and South Carolina become two separate colonies.

1715 Hundreds of Native Americans and settlers die in the Yamasee War.

1718 Blackbeard terrorizes merchant ships approaching the Carolina coast.

1719 South Carolina becomes a royal colony.

1739 Slaves revolt in the Stono Rebellion.

1765 South Carolina residents protest the Stamp Act.

1775 The Revolutionary War begins.

1776 All 13 American Colonies formally declare their independence from Great Britain on July 4.

1780 British soldiers capture Charles Town. Americans win the Battle of Kings Mountain.

1781 In January the Patriots win an important victory at the Battle of Cowpens.

1783 The Americans and British sign the Treaty of Paris, officially ending the Revolutionary War.

1788 South Carolina ratifies the Constitution and becomes the eighth state of the new United States.

Regions of the 13 Colonies		
Northern Colonies	**Middle Colonies**	**Southern Colonies**
Connecticut, Massachusetts, New Hampshire, Rhode Island	Delaware, New Jersey, New York, Pennsylvania	Georgia, Maryland, North Carolina, South Carolina, Virginia
land more suitable for hunting than farming; trees cut down for lumber; trapped wild animals for their meat and fur; fished in rivers, lakes, and ocean	the "Breadbasket" colonies—rich farmland, perfect for growing wheat, corn, rye, and other grains	soil better for growing tobacco, rice, and indigo; crops grown on huge farms called plantations; landowners depended heavily on servants and slaves to work in the fields

Glossary

baptize (BAP-tyz)—to admit into the Christian faith with a spiritual ceremony

boycott (BOY-kot)—to refuse to buy or use a product or service to protest something believed to be wrong or unfair

cash crop (KASH KROP)—a crop that is grown to be sold rather than for use by the farmer

epidemic (e-puh-DE-mik)—an infectious disease that spreads quickly through a community or population group

guerilla warfare (gur-RIL-lah WOR-fair)—a type of military action using small groups of fighters to carry out surprise attacks against enemy forces

immigrant (IM-uh-gruhnt)—a person who moves from one country to live permanently in another

Loyalist (LOI-uh-list)—a colonist who was loyal to Great Britain during the Revolutionary War

militia (muh-LISH-uh)—a group of volunteer citizens who are organized to fight but are not professional soldiers

natural resource (NACH-ur-uhl REE-sorss)—something in nature that people use, such as coal and trees

Parliament (PAR-luh-muhnt)—Great Britain's lawmaking body

Patriot (PAY-tree-uht)—a person who sided with the colonies during the Revolutionary War

persecute (PUR-suh-kyoot)—to continually treat in a cruel and unfair way

plantation (plan-TAY-shuhn)—a large farm where crops are grown

prey (PRAY)—an animal hunted by another animal for food

proprietor (proh-PREYE-uh-ter)—a person given ownership of a colony

ratify (RAT-uh-fye)—to formally approve a document

repeal (ri-PEEL)—to officially cancel something, such as a law

royal colony (ROI-uhl KAH-luh-nee)—a colony controlled by a monarch

smallpox (SMAWL-poks)—a disease that spreads easily from person to person, causing chills, fever, and pimples that scar

suffocate (SUHF-uh-kate)—to die from a lack of air or oxygen

yellow fever (YEL-oh FEE-vur)—an illness that can cause high fever, chills, nausea, and kidney and liver failure; liver failure causes the skin to become yellow, giving the disease its name.

Critical Thinking Using the Common Core

1. Compare and contrast the various reasons that people from other colonies and Europe settled in South Carolina. (Integration of Knowledge and Ideas).

2. Do you think the colonists were justified in protesting the taxes placed on them to pay for the French and Indian War? Why or why not? Use details from the text to support your answer. (Key Ideas and Details)

3. Review Chapter 6 "Life in Colonial South Carolina." Then compare and contrast life in Colonial times to life now. (Craft and structure)

Read More

Buckley, James, Jr. *Who Was Blackbeard?* New York: Grosset & Dunlap, 2015.

Jeffries, Joyce. *The Colony of South Carolina*. Spotlight on the 13 Colonies. New York: PowerKids Press, 2015.

Micklos, John, Jr. *The Making of the United States from Thirteen Colonies—Through Primary Sources*. The American Revolution Through Primary Sources. Berkeley Heights, N.J.: Enslow Publishers, 2013.

Moss, Marissa. *America's Tea Parties: Not One but Four! Boston, Charleston, New York, Philadelphia*. New York: Abrams Books for Young Readers, 2016.

Pratt, Mary K. *A Timeline History of the Thirteen Colonies*. Timeline Trackers: America's Beginnings. Minneapolis: Lerner Publications, 2014.

Internet Sites

FactHound offers a safe, fun way to find Internet sites related to this book. All of the sites on FactHound have been researched by our staff.
Here's all you do:
Visit *www.facthound.com*
Type in this code: 9781515722304

 Check out projects, games and lots more at
www.capstonekids.com

Source Notes

Page 15, callout quote: Hugh Talmage Lefler, ed. "A Description of 'Carolana' by a 'Well-Willer,' 1649." *North Carolina Historical Review*, Volume XXXII Numbers 1–4 (1955): 103. Accessed February 2, 2016. https://archive.org/stream/northcarolinahis1955nort/northcarolinahis1955nort_djvu.txt.

Page 16, callout quote: William Hilton. *A Relation of a Discovery Lately Made on the Coast of Florida*. London: Printed by J.C. for Simon Miller, 1664, p. 13. Accessed February 2, 2016. http://quod.lib.umich.edu/e/eebo/A43838.0001.001/1:4?rgn=div1;view=fulltext.

Page 20, callout quote: Edward McCrady. *The History of South Carolina Under the Proprietary Government, 1670–1719*. New York: The Macmillan Company, 1897, p. 308. Accessed February 2, 2016. https://archive.org/stream/historyofsouthca00mcc#page/308/mode/2up.

Page 22, callout quote: Charles Johnson. *A General History of the Pyrates…* London: T. Warner, 1724, p. 87. Accessed February 2, 2016. https://archive.org/stream/generalhistoryof00defo#page/86/mode/2up.

Page 26, callout quote: Walter Edgar. *South Carolina: A History*. Columbia, S.C.: University of South Carolina Press, 1998, p. 162.

Page 27, callout quote: Eliza Lucas Pinckney. *The Letterbook of Eliza Lucas Pinckney, 1739–1762*. Edited by Elise Pinckney. Chapel Hill, N.C.: University of North Carolina Press, 1972, p. 16.

Page 30, callout quote: Schöpf, Johann David. *Travels in the Confederation (1783–1784)*. Translated and edited by Alfred J. Morrison. Philadelphia: William J. Campbell, 1911, p. 147. Accessed February 2, 2016. https://archive.org/stream/travelsinconfede02schp/travelsinconfede02schp_djvu.txt.

Page 37, primary source box: "Charleston Tea Party." *South Carolina Gazette*. Page 2. November 21,1774. Charleston Library Society, Charleston, S.C. Accessed February 2, 2016. http://www.teachingushistory.org/CharlestonTeaPartyarticleintheSouthCarolinaGazetteNovember211774.html#Transcription.

Page 39, line 11: Thomas Jefferson. "From Thomas Jefferson to John Campbell, November 10, 1822," Founders Online, National Archives. Accessed February 2, 2016. http://founders.archives.gov/documents/Jefferson/98-01-02-3152.

Select Bibliography

Edgar, Walter. *South Carolina: A History*. Columbia, S.C.: University of South Carolina Press, 1998.

Gallay, Alan. *Colonial Wars of North America, 1512–1763: An Encyclopedia*. New York: Garland Publishing, 1996.

Gallay, Alan. *The Indian Slave Trade: The Rise of the English Empire in the American South*. New Haven, Conn.: Yale University Press, 2002.

Hilton, William. *A Relation of a Discovery Lately Made on the Coast of Florida*. London: Printed by J.C. for Simon Miller, 1664.

Jameson, John Franklin, ed. *Original Narratives of Early American History*, Volume 11. New York: Charles Scribner's Sons, 1906.

Johnson, Charles. *A General History of the Pyrates…* London: T. Warner, 1724.

Lee, Robert E., *Blackbeard the Pirate: A Reappraisal of His Life and Times*. Winston-Salem, N.C.: John F. Blair, 1974.

McCrady, Edward. *The History of South Carolina Under the Proprietary Government, 1670–1719*. New York: The Macmillan Company, 1897.

Pinckney, Eliza Lucas. *The Letterbook of Eliza Lucas Pinckney, 1739–1762*. Edited by Elise Pinckney. Chapel Hill, N.C.: University of North Carolina Press, 1972.

Salley, Alexander Samuel. *Narratives of Early Carolina, 1650–1708*, Volume 12. New York: Charles Scribner's Sons, 1911.

Schöpf, Johann David. *Travels in the Confederation (1783–1784)*. Translated and edited by Alfred J. Morrison. Philadelphia: William J. Campbell, 1911.

Index